CORE LIBRARY OF US STATES

New Jersey

BY HELEN EVANS WALSH

CONTENT CONSULTANT
Jonathan Mercantini, PhD
Dean, College of Liberal Arts
Kean University

Core Library

An Imprint of Abdo Publishing
abdobooks.com

abdobooks.com

Published by Abdo Publishing, a division of ABDO, PO Box 398166, Minneapolis, Minnesota 55439.

Printed in the United States of America, North Mankato, Minnesota.
052022
092022

THIS BOOK CONTAINS RECYCLED MATERIALS

Cover Photo: Shutterstock Images
Interior Photos: Vlad G./Shutterstock Images, 4–5; Red Line Editorial, 8 (New Jersey), 8 (USA); T Photography/Shutterstock Images, 9, 43; MyLoupe/Universal Images Group/Getty Images, 10–11; Education Images/Glasshouse Vintage/Universal History Archive/Universal Images Group/Getty Images, 13; Comet Design/Shutterstock Images, 17 (flag); Pawel Horazy/Shutterstock Images, 17 (tree); Shutterstock Images, 17 (flower), 17 (bird), 23, 27, 39, 40; Andrew Julian Photography/Shutterstock Images, 17 (fish); Real Window Creative/Shutterstock Images, 19, 45; Mihai Andritoiu/Shutterstock Images, 20–21, 28–29, 37; Erin Cadigan/Shutterstock Images, 25; Olivier Le Queinec/Shutterstock Images, 31; Fin Costello/Redferns/Getty Images, 34–35

Editor: Arnold Ringstad
Series Designer: Joshua Olson

Library of Congress Control Number: 2021951391

Publisher's Cataloging-in-Publication Data

Names: Evans Walsh, Helen, author.
Title: New Jersey / by Helen Evans Walsh
Description: Minneapolis, Minnesota : Abdo Publishing, 2023 | Series: Core library of US states | Includes online resources and index.
Identifiers: ISBN 9781532197710 (lib. bdg.) | ISBN 9781098270476 (ebook)
Subjects: LCSH: U.S. states--Juvenile literature. | Northeastern States--Juvenile literature. | New Jersey--History--Juvenile literature. | Physical geography--United States--Juvenile literature.
Classification: DDC 974.9--dc23

Population demographics broken down by race and ethnicity come from the 2019 census estimate. Population totals come from the 2020 census.

CONTENTS

T-SHIRT
FACTORY
ATM
PIZZA

CHAPTER ONE

THE GARDEN STATE

The summer sun warms the planks of the Ocean City boardwalk. The smell of the salty sea air combines with the savory scent of pizza and French fries. Overhead, seagulls squawk. A family descends the boardwalk stairs onto the sandy beach. The children gaze excitedly at the blue-green ocean waves lapping at the shore. They dig their toes into the warm sand.

Ocean City is a town located near the southern end of New Jersey. It is one of

New Jersey's Ocean City boardwalk is filled with places to eat, have fun, and relax.

New Jersey's most famous places. Families have been vacationing in Ocean City for generations. It is known for its sandy beaches. It is also known for its nearly 2.5-mile (4-km) boardwalk. On the boardwalk, visitors will find shops and restaurants. Many people enjoy the boardwalk's carnival rides and games.

PERSPECTIVES

TOURISM AND THE JERSEY SHORE

Around 48 million visitors traveled to the New Jersey shore in 2019. Most visitors come to the shore during the peak summer months. Many New Jersey residents and businesses rely on the income the tourists provide. Even so, residents also enjoy the quieter times after the tourists leave. Dot Tochterman has lived in Ocean City for more than 25 years. She compares tourists to house guests. In 2017 she said, "You're happy to see them come, but you're also happy to see them go."

ABOUT NEW JERSEY

New Jersey is part of the northeast region of the United States. Its eastern coast lies on the Atlantic Ocean. The state borders New York to the north and Pennsylvania to the west. The Delaware

River separates New Jersey from Delaware in the southwest.

New Jersey is known as the Garden State. It got this nickname in the 1800s. The true origins of the nickname are unclear. Today the state is home to many people. It is the most densely populated US state. Many people live in a relatively small area.

NEW JERSEY'S NICKNAME

Abraham Browning of Camden is often credited with giving New Jersey its nickname. Browning served as the state's attorney general from 1845 to 1850. In 1876 Browning spoke at an event in Philadelphia, Pennsylvania. During his speech, he supposedly called New Jersey "our Garden State." Later research showed that he never used the phrase. Still, people passed around false stories about the speech. The nickname stuck. In 1954 the New Jersey state legislature passed a bill to add "The Garden State" to car license plates.

Newark and Jersey City are close to New York City. Asbury Park, Ocean City, and Cape May have vibrant beach communities. People go there to relax

MAP OF NEW JERSEY

New Jersey has a long shoreline. In what ways do you think the shore is important to the people of New Jersey?

The New Jersey Turnpike carries motorists to destinations across the state.

in the sun or party downtown at night. Atlantic City is home to several casinos and resorts.

The New Jersey Turnpike is one of the busiest highways in the country. Every day, hundreds of thousands of vehicles travel on the road. The turnpike runs from the northeast corner of the state to the southwest. It is part of the highway system that goes from Maine in the north to Miami, Florida, in the south. People who live in New Jersey often use it to reach nearby states such as New York and Pennsylvania. Still, people can easily leave bustling urban and suburban areas to enjoy nature in the Garden State too.

CHAPTER TWO

HISTORY OF NEW JERSEY

Beginning at least 10,000 years ago, the Lenape (Delaware) people lived in the New Jersey region. They settled along the Delaware River. Large communities lived together to farm in the summer months. During winters, they broke into smaller family groups. Families traveled around to hunt and fish. By the 1600s, 30 to 40 large Lenape communities lived in the area that would become New Jersey.

Modern reconstructions show the types of structures, called wigwams, that Lenape people used in the past.

EUROPEANS ARRIVE

In 1524 the first European explorers came to what is now New Jersey. They began settling in towns. During the 1600s, Indigenous peoples from nearby states fled to New Jersey. Some tried to escape violence from other tribes. Some were pushed off their lands by white settlers. However, these incoming Indigenous peoples competed with the Lenape for land. This led to fights between the Lenape and other peoples such as the Susquehannock.

The Lenape were kind to white settlers at first. But the Europeans did not treat them fairly. In the late 1600s, the Lenape sold land to people from England. But the English often didn't pay them. Eventually the land became an English colony. In 1664 the English gave the area the name New Jersey. They named it after the English Channel's Isle of Jersey.

White settlement took a toll on American Indian nations. They struggled and fought to retain their lands.

George Washington commanded American troops at the Battle of Trenton.

But most American Indian nations ultimately lost lands. Many people died from European diseases. Some were enslaved by white settlers.

REVOLUTION AND STATEHOOD

European settlements continued to grow. In 1756 the College of New Jersey opened in Princeton. It was later renamed Princeton University. It is the oldest college in the state. Iron mining increased. New Jersey factories made weapons for soldiers during the American Revolutionary War (1775–1783). During that war, people living in the American colonies fought for independence from Great Britain. One of the war's key battles, the Battle of Trenton, was fought on December 26, 1776. The colonists eventually won the war. They formed the United States of America.

New Jersey became the third US state on December 18, 1787. In 1789 it was the first state to adopt the Bill of Rights. This document lists some of the basic rights of Americans. As a new state, New Jersey focused on rebuilding from damage done during the war.

GROWTH OF CITIES

Companies built factories in New Jersey cities in the 1800s. Paterson produced fabrics. Trenton produced iron and steel. Railroads helped carry goods out of New Jersey. Immigrants came from Europe to work in the new factories. The population of New Jersey grew.

Slavery became a major political issue throughout the country in the 1800s. Black people had been enslaved in New Jersey starting in the 1600s. New laws gradually ended slavery in the state in the early 1800s. It was fully outlawed in New Jersey in 1846.

Starting in 1860 some states in the South broke away from the United States. They wanted to keep the practice of slavery. The northern states, called the Union, wanted to hold the country together. The two sides fought in the American Civil War (1861–1865). New Jersey was part of the Union. More than 25,000 men from New Jersey joined the fighting. The Union won the war, and slavery became illegal throughout the country. Still, Black

FROM DIRT TO MEDICINE

Selman Waksman studied soil at New Jersey's Rutgers University in the early 1900s. At that time, tuberculosis (TB) was a common and deadly disease. It killed up to 400 people a day in the United States. Scientists searched for medicine to treat TB. Waksman decided to look at dirt for the answer. It was an unusual research idea. But Waksman believed bacteria in soil could help. He was right. He helped make the first TB antibiotic medicine. The number of TB deaths dropped.

people in New Jersey and across the nation continued to face discrimination and inequality.

PERSPECTIVES

TRAFFIC ON THE TURNPIKE

The New Jersey Turnpike is one of the busiest roads in the United States. Travelers often encounter traffic and congestion on the highway. Some people think that widening the turnpike will lessen the traffic. However, others, including Jeff Tittel, director of the New Jersey Sierra Club, believe that widening the turnpike will only cause more problems. In 2021 he said, "When you widen roads, you increase traffic and just move the bottleneck from one place to another."

New Jersey's economy changed as its population continued to grow. Cities boomed. People cleared farmland to make room for homes and businesses. The New Jersey Turnpike opened in 1951. Thousands of people had new options for traveling. The highway became crowded. More lanes were added over time. As more and more people owned cars, it became easier

NEW JERSEY
QUICK FACTS

Many things make New Jersey unique. How do these facts and statistics help you better understand the state?

Abbreviation: NJ
Nickname: The Garden State
Motto: Liberty and prosperity
Date of statehood: December 18, 1787
Capital: Trenton
Population: 9,288,994
Area: 8,723 square miles (22,591 sq km)

STATE SYMBOLS

State bird
Eastern goldfinch

State flower
Violet

State fish
Brook trout

State tree
Red oak

to live in suburbs and commute to cities for work. New Jersey's suburbs expanded.

NEW JERSEY GOVERNMENT

Today New Jersey's government has three branches. No branch is more powerful than the others. The legislative branch writes bills. Two groups form this branch. The Senate has 40 members. The General Assembly has 80 members. The executive branch is led by the governor. The governor signs bills into law. The judicial branch is the court system.

New Jersey does not have any federally recognized American Indian tribes. But three tribes are recognized by the state. This allows them to qualify for benefits from the state government. Each tribe has lived in New Jersey for hundreds of years. The Nanticoke Lenni-Lenape Tribal Nation is the largest tribe in the state. A council of nine leaders governs the tribe. Its community center is located in Fairfield Township. The Ramapough Lenape Nation lives in the Ramapo

The capitol building in Trenton sits along the Delaware River.

Mountains. The Ramapough Lenape people are also known as the Keepers of the Pass. The people of the Powhatan Renape Nation live in northeast New Jersey.

EXPLORE ONLINE

Chapter Two discusses the Lenape people. The website below goes into more depth on this topic. Does the website answer any questions you had about the Lenape?

THE NANTICOKE LENNI-LENAPE

abdocorelibrary.com/new-jersey

CHAPTER THREE

GEOGRAPHY AND CLIMATE

New Jersey may be small in land area, but that doesn't limit the different types of environments found there. The state has several distinct geographic areas. The Valley and Ridge region makes up the northwest. The Appalachian Mountains run through the state here. The region includes High Point, New Jersey's highest peak at 1,803 feet (550 m) above sea level. The southwest region is mainly highlands. Pine forests grow here.

A monument dedicated to veterans marks High Point in northern New Jersey.

A plateau covers the central part of the state. It is mostly flat with occasional rolling hills. More cities are located here than in the mountains. Some of the state's most fertile land is on the plateau. Near the ocean, the coastal plain slopes down to the water. The soil becomes sandy near the shore. In the northeast, some marshes and swamps border the water. Wild grasses grow in the wetlands.

One reason New Jersey has fertile soil is that it has many water sources. There are nearly 1,000 bodies of water in the state. They include rivers, lakes, and streams. New Jersey's Atlantic coastline stretches more than 100 miles (160 km). The state's weather changes greatly between seasons. Summers are warm and humid. Winters are cold and snowy.

PLANTS AND WILDLIFE

Many types of plants and animals live in New Jersey. They thrive in different habitats, from the coast to

New Jersey experiences snowy and icy conditions in the winter.

the mountains. Birches, hemlocks, and sweetgum trees grow in forests. So do oaks, including the state tree, the red oak. Colorful flowers bloom throughout the state. They include wild azaleas, rhododendrons, and New Jersey's state flower, the violet.

The knobbed whelk snail crawls along beaches and bays. Ospreys build nests in grasses on sandy dunes. The bright-yellow eastern goldfinch, the state bird, lives in New Jersey's woodlands and visits backyard feeders. Mammals such as rabbits, squirrels, and white-tailed deer also call the state home.

However, wild habitats shrank as cities expanded.

BROOK TROUT

The brook trout is New Jersey's state fish. The trout's body is spotted. These fish live mainly in streams and rivers, though some adults migrate to the ocean. Brook trout are important indicator animals. This means scientists can study them to learn about the health of the environment. If water is healthy, brook trout thrive. If water is polluted, they do not.

White-tailed deer are among the animals that can be spotted in New Jersey's wilderness.

Bears, deer, raccoons, and other animals are sometimes seen in people's neighborhoods. They have nowhere else to go. Some areas are set aside for wildlife. The government protects the Great Swamp National Wildlife

Refuge in northeast New Jersey. This area covers 7,800 acres (3,200 ha). It is home to a variety of birds, mammals, reptiles, and amphibians. Hiking trails give visitors a chance to see these species up close. People can photograph and learn about the refuge's wildlife. The government prevents companies from building homes and businesses in this part of New Jersey.

Habitat loss isn't the only threat to New Jersey wildlife. Climate change puts wildlife and people at risk.

PERSPECTIVES

ENDANGERED SPECIES

New Jersey is home to more than 700 endangered species. Loss of habitat is one of the major threats to their survival. The Nature Conservancy (TNC) is a global nonprofit working to protect endangered species and their habitats. Their nature preserves throughout the state provide safe homes for many species. "Our preserves offer quality habitat," says Eric Olsen of TNC's New Jersey branch. "Often the sites are away from roads and development, and provide the right forest, field and water resources to give wildlife the best chance for survival."

Many businesses and homes in New Jersey sit near the water, putting them at risk from rising sea levels.

Climate change causes sea levels to rise, leading to flooding. This may wash away some of New Jersey's coastal habitats.

FURTHER EVIDENCE

Chapter Three discusses how the growth of cities has impacted New Jersey's plants and animals. Identify one of the author's main points. What evidence does the author provide to support this point? The website at the link below also discusses this topic. Find a quote on this website that supports the author's main point. Does it offer a new piece of evidence?

BACKYARD WILDLIFE HABITATS IN NEW JERSEY

abdocorelibrary.com/new-jersey

CHAPTER FOUR

RESOURCES AND ECONOMY

Because of its location, New Jersey has always been an important transportation hub. After the American Civil War, the state became a central stop on US railroad lines. Manufacturing was one of New Jersey's first big industries. It had access to raw materials and many workers. Today manufacturing remains an important part of New Jersey's economy. In 2019 about 250,000 people worked in manufacturing jobs.

New Jersey's major cities, including Newark, are densely packed with commercial and industrial companies.

Many of them worked in factories that produce chemical, electronic, and food products.

New Jersey's service and technology industries have become major parts of the state's economy. Service industries include education, health care, tourism, and financial services. New Jersey is also a major research center. It has many scientists and engineers. These people work for pharmaceutical companies, biotechnology companies, and life sciences companies. Some work for companies that make electronics, computers,

THOMAS EDISON

One of the United States' most famous inventors, Thomas Edison, worked in New Jersey. Edison built his famous research laboratory in Menlo Park in 1876. There Edison conducted research that led to many of his most well-known inventions. He invented a new electric light bulb and the phonograph. He also invented motion-picture technology. By the time Edison died in 1931, he held 1,093 patents covering his inventions.

Cranberries are usually harvested from bogs in New Jersey in October.

and medical devices. The state's huge transportation system provides lots of jobs too.

Farming remains a small but important part of New Jersey's economy. Less than 1 percent of workers are farmers. Horse farms are located in the state's south and central areas. Dairy farms are located in the northwest valleys. People cut lumber from forests.

They catch shellfish near Cape May. They grow blueberries, cranberries, bell peppers, and tomatoes.

Many people who live in New Jersey work in another state. Major companies in New York and Pennsylvania are nearby. Huge numbers of commuters take the turnpike. Others ride trains from New Jersey into neighboring states.

PERSPECTIVES

WOMEN IN FARMING

In New Jersey, a growing number of farmers are women. Emily Hennelly of Bedminster is one of New Jersey's female farmers. Hennelly owns AnyThyme Farm. She grows a variety of flowers and herbs. When her flowers are in season, she gets up at 4:00 a.m. every day to work. She says, "The hours are crazy, especially in the summer, and while every year we grow and do better financially, it can be hard to justify all the work that goes into it. But I love it and get so much out of it."

STRAIGHT TO THE SOURCE

In September 2020 the state of New Jersey released a report about its economy. The report mentioned how the state's modern economy was affected by the COVID-19 pandemic:

> *Reflecting a nationwide trend, the New Jersey economy has trended toward more of a service-providing blend of industries from one based on the production of goods. By 2020 in New Jersey, more than 90 percent of all employment was found in service-providing industries. This fact may have [worsened] the deep losses felt in spring when social distancing became of paramount importance, as these are the types of jobs where close human interaction is a critical part of one's job responsibilities.*

Source: "Economic Brief: New Jersey's Changing Economy and the Recent Impact of the COVID-19 Pandemic." *New Jersey Department of Labor and Workforce Development*, Sept. 2020, nj.gov. Accessed 3 Aug. 2021.

CONSIDER YOUR AUDIENCE

Review this passage closely. Consider how you would adapt it for a different audience, such as your friends. Write a blog post conveying this same information so that it can be understood by them. How does your new approach differ from the original and why?

CHAPTER FIVE

PEOPLE AND PLACES

Famous New Jerseyans include basketball superstar Shaquille O'Neal, actor John Travolta, and astronaut Buzz Aldrin, who was the second person to walk on the moon. Rappers and actors Queen Latifah and Ice-T are both from the Garden State. So is famed singer Whitney Houston. Musicians Jon Bon Jovi and Bruce Springsteen are both from New Jersey too. Springsteen has written several songs about his home state.

Rocker Bruce Springsteen performs in New Jersey in 1975.

NEW JERSEY DEMOGRAPHICS

In 2020 more than 9.2 million people lived in New Jersey. White people who are not Hispanic or Latino made up a little more than half of the population. The next largest groups were Hispanic or Latino at about 20 percent and Black at about 15 percent.

New Jersey has a large immigrant population. Almost one quarter of the state's people were born in another country. These immigrants have helped shape the state. In 2018 the largest share of New Jersey's immigrants came from India, making up 13 percent. Other common countries included the Dominican Republic and Mexico.

SUPERSTAR SINGER

Whitney Houston was born in Newark. Her mother was a famous singer. Her cousins sang too. Houston's family helped her discover her love of music. As a teen, she performed in New York. By age 22, her music career took off. She became one of the most popular female artists in history.

The city of Dover has a large Hispanic population.

Most people in New Jersey live and work in the state's northern cities. Only one-fourth of the population lives south of Trenton. There are many wealthy residents. In 2019 New Jersey had a higher percentage of millionaires than any other state. But New Jersey struggles with poverty too. In many cities, old buildings and factories are falling out of use. Some people have been moving out of cities and into suburbs.

HAVING FUN IN THE GARDEN STATE

There is a lot to see and do in New Jersey. The New Jersey Devils hockey team plays there. Several New York sports teams actually play in New Jersey. These include the New York Giants, New York Jets, and New York Red Bulls. There are national parks and nature preserves such as the Pine Barrens. People camp, hike, canoe, and explore these places. Many people vacation at New Jersey's sandy beaches. Some people visit the casinos in Atlantic City.

Many people visit New Jersey for its art. People can tour the Montclair Art Museum.

PERSPECTIVES

THE PINE BARRENS

New Jersey's Pine Barrens is a popular place for people who enjoy outdoor adventures. The Pine Barrens covers 1.1 million acres (0.45 million ha) in New Jersey. Brian Parker of Mount Holly, New Jersey, enjoys exploring the Pine Barrens. He says, "I'm drawn to it all the time. And when I can bring people out there, I do. Like a friend of mine this last Saturday, it was his first time out there. . . . Out of nowhere he says, 'Now I get it.' . . . It's pretty enchanting."

The USS *New Jersey* museum ship is a popular destination.

They can see a show at the performing arts center in Newark. The Nanticoke Lenni-Lenape Tribal Nation has its headquarters in Bridgeton. A shop there sells arts and crafts made by members of the tribal nation.

Other people visit New Jersey to learn about its place in American history. New Jersey has more than 250 historic sites. Camden is where the first US drive-in movie theater opened. The USS *New Jersey*

The resort town of Cape May has been a top tourist spot for many decades.

battleship museum is also located in Camden. In Cape May, visitors tour historic Victorian houses and the Cape May Lighthouse. New Jersey's big cities, beautiful landscapes, and rich history offer something for everyone.

STRAIGHT TO THE **SOURCE**

In 2021 National Public Radio interviewer Terry Gross spoke to Bruce Springsteen. She asked him about why he chose to stay in New Jersey after becoming famous. Springsteen said:

> *I just felt very comfortable here. And I was uncomfortable with city life. I was more or less a kid that came out of a small town. And I was a beach bum and loved the ocean and loved the sun and I liked the people that were here. I liked who I was when I was here. I wanted to continue writing about the things that I felt were important, and those things were pretty much here. I felt like a lot of my heroes from the past lost themselves in different ways once they had a certain amount of success. And I was nervous about that. And I wanted to remain grounded. And living in this part of New Jersey was something that was—it was essential to who I was and continues, to this day, to be that way.*

Source: Terry Gross. "Bruce Springsteen: On Jersey, Masculinity and Wishing to Be His Stage Persona." *NPR*, 2 July 2021, npr.org. Accessed 22 July 2021.

WHAT'S THE BIG IDEA?

Read the above answer carefully. What is the main point Springsteen is trying to make? Name two or three details he uses to support his main idea.

IMPORTANT DATES

About 10,000 years ago
Lenape people begin living in the New Jersey area.

1524 CE
The first European explorers come to New Jersey.

1756
The College of New Jersey opens in Princeton, New Jersey. It is later renamed Princeton University.

1787
New Jersey becomes the third US state on December 18.

1789
New Jersey is the first state to adopt the Bill of Rights.

1861–1865
Troops from New Jersey fight for the Union in the American Civil War.

1951

The New Jersey Turnpike opens.

2020s

The New Jersey Turnpike is one of the busiest highways in the United States.

STOP AND THINK

Tell the Tale

Chapter Three describes New Jersey's natural landscapes, and Chapter Two discusses how many factories were built in the state in the 1800s. How do you think the new factories and growing cities changed New Jersey's landscapes? Write a paragraph describing how these developments might have changed the look of the state.

Surprise Me

Chapter Four discusses the economy of New Jersey. After reading this book, what two or three facts about New Jersey's economy did you find most surprising? Write a few sentences about each fact. Why did you find each fact surprising?

Take a Stand

Many people believe that building new cities and roads is good for a community. Others are concerned about how this construction affects natural habitats. Do you think expanding cities is helpful, harmful, or both? Why?

Why Do I Care?

You may not have visited all of New Jersey's geographic regions. But that doesn't mean you can't think about what they mean for the state. Why are New Jersey's regions important to the state? Why is it important to protect them?

GLOSSARY

antibiotic
a medicine designed to kill microorganisms, such as bacteria

climate change
a human-caused global crisis involving long-term changes in Earth's temperature and weather patterns

colony
an area of land that is separate from but controlled by another country

commute
to travel a distance to work or school every day, usually by car, bus, or train

enslaved
held as a slave

fertile
rich in nutrients for growing plants

habitat
the place where a plant or an animal lives

plateau
high, flat land

polluted
dirty or impure, especially due to industrial waste or other products produced by humans

ONLINE RESOURCES

To learn more about New Jersey, visit our free resource websites below.

Core Library CONNECTION
FREE! COMMON CORE MULTIMEDIA RESOURCES

Visit **abdocorelibrary.com** or scan this QR code for free Common Core resources for teachers and students, including vetted activities, multimedia, and booklinks, for deeper subject comprehension.

Booklinks NONFICTION NETWORK
FREE! ONLINE NONFICTION RESOURCES

Visit **abdobooklinks.com** or scan this QR code for free additional online weblinks for further learning. These links are routinely monitored and updated to provide the most current information available.

LEARN MORE

Gale, Ryan. *Fact and Fiction of the Civil War*. Abdo, 2021.

Miller, Derek. *New Jersey*. Cavendish Square, 2020.

INDEX

About the Author

Helen Evans Walsh is the author of several books for young adults and children. She lives in Pittsburgh, Pennsylvania, with her husband and children. For many years, she has enjoyed family vacations at New Jersey's beaches and boardwalks.